THE DEATH OF SITTING BEAR

Praise for N. Scott Momaday
and *The Death of Sitting Bear*

"These are the poems of a master poet, born of an age when our ears were not so bent toward digital production. Or should I say, these are the poems of a bear who has walked through several generations and stands before us, breathing clouds into a cold dawn, bearing this book of poetry. The bear's journey is mythic, a migration through tragedy and beauty, over lands rich with horses and stories. When you read these poems, you will learn to hear deeply the sound a soul makes as it sings about the mystery of dreaming and becoming."

—Joy Harjo, Muscogee Nation, US Poet Laureate

"An admirable capstone to a distinguished literary career . . . a treasure for Momaday's readers and an excellent introduction for those new to Native American writing."

—*Library Journal* (starred review)

"[Momaday] is at root a storyteller who both preserves and expands Native American culture in his critically praised, transformative writing." —Henry Louis Gates Jr.

"[A] generous collection. . . . Each poem reflects a lifetime of writing across the intersections of history, identity, and language. This accessible compendium allows readers to savor the life's work of an unparalleled poet."

—*Booklist*

"Firmly steeped in Kiowa heritage and indigenous oral storytelling traditions, Momaday breathes in the spirit of the Southwest and breathes out masterful imagery onto the page. The poems beg to be read aloud in order to savor the taste of the language, each word carefully chosen to evoke shape, sound, sight, feeling, and history with the weight of its intention. . . . This incredibly personal collection of poems presents deep reflections on the natural world, indigenous history, and the nature of humans, animals, and God."

—*Shelf Awareness* (starred review)

"Momaday . . . must be ranked among the greatest of our contemporary writers and our environmental prophets."

—*American Scholar*

"The single best collection of works from a master of Native letters."   —*TCJ Student*

"Momaday [is] an important voice in American letters."

—*Los Angeles Times*

"A gem of a collection. . . . Soulful, heartfelt, beautifully constructed, and technically brilliant, this is a book written by one of our most important and unique voices."

—*Fjords Review*

"To read Momaday is to read the land. It is to encounter the earth alive with wind and sunlight, with plants and animals, and to know all of it—each aspect of the world—by name. It is also to renew a reverence for beauty and a feeling of hope."   —*Stanford Magazine*

ALSO BY N. SCOTT MOMADAY

Poetry

Dream Drawings: Configurations of a Timeless Kind

Again the Far Morning: New and Selected Poems

In the Presence of the Sun: Stories and Poems, 1961–1991

The Gourd Dancer

Angle of Geese and Other Poems

Novels

The Ancient Child

House Made of Dawn

Other Works

Earth Keeper: Reflections on the American Land

*Three Plays: The Indolent Boys, Children of the Sun,
and The Moon in Two Windows*

Four Arrows & Magpie: A Kiowa Story

In the Bear's House

The Man Made of Words: Essays, Stories, Passages

Circle of Wonder: A Native American Christmas Story

The Names: A Memoir

The Way to Rainy Mountain

The Journey of Tai-Me

The

DEATH

of

SITTING
BEAR

NEW AND SELECTED POEMS

N. Scott Momaday

HARPER ● PERENNIAL

NEW YORK ● LONDON ● TORONTO ● SYDNEY ● NEW DELHI ● AUCKLAND

HARPER ⬤ PERENNIAL

A hardcover edition of this book was published in 2020 by
Harper, an Imprint of HarperCollins Publishers.

THE DEATH OF SITTING BEAR: NEW AND SELECTED POEMS. Copyright © 2020
by N. Scott Momaday. All rights reserved. Printed in the United States
of America. No part of this book may be used or reproduced in any
manner whatsoever without written permission except in the case of brief
quotations embodied in critical articles and reviews. For information,
address HarperCollins Publishers, 195 Broadway, New York, NY 10007.

HarperCollins books may be purchased for educational, business,
or sales promotional use. For information, please email the Special Markets
Department at SPsales@harpercollins.com.

FIRST HARPER PERENNIAL EDITION PUBLISHED 2022.

Excerpt from the poem "Esse" by Czeslaw Milosz from
Selected and Last Poems: 1931–2004 by Czeslaw Milosz.
Copyright © 1988, 1991, 1995, 2001, 2004, 2006 by The Czeslaw
Milosz Estate. Courtesy of HarperCollins Publishers.

All artwork by N. Scott Momaday

Designed by Bonni Leon-Berman

Library of Congress Cataloging-in-Publication Data

Names: Momaday, N. Scott, 1934– author.
Title: The death of sitting bear : new and selected poems /
N. Scott Momaday.
Description: First edition. | New York, NY : Harper, an imprint
of HarperCollinsPublishers, [2020]
Identifiers: LCCN 2019034730 | ISBN 9780062961150 (hardcover) |
ISBN 9780062961167 (paperback)
Classification: LCC PS3563.O47 A6 2020 | DDC 813/.54—dc23
LC record available at https://lccn.loc.gov/2019034730

24 25 26 27 28 LBC 6 5 4 3 2

To the memory of Yvor Winters

CONTENTS

PART II

PART III

PREFACE

The poems in this book reflect my deep respect for and appreciation of words. I consider myself especially fortunate to have been given a rich sampling of storytelling as a child. My mother was well versed in English literature, and she taught me how to discover the wealth within books. My father, who was a Native American of the Kiowa tribe and whose first language was unwritten, told me stories from the Kiowa oral tradition.

I became a poet. I believe poetry is the highest form of verbal expression. Although I have written in other forms, I find that poems are what I want and need most to read and write. They give life to my mind.

I have a recurrent dream. In it there is a child who lives hundreds of years ago in a village in Anglo-Saxon England. Early one morning the child is awakened by its parents, who whisk the child away into the forest. There, around a clearing, are gathered the people of the village. They chatter with excitement, and the child does not know what is happening. Then a little old man, dressed in a ragged robe and hood, steps into the clearing, and a hush falls on the scene. The old man begins to speak, "Hwaet we Gar-Dena in geardagum . . ." And he recites *Beowulf*, the oldest poem in the English (Old English) language. It is a long recitation, of some 3,182 metrical lines, but no one turns away. It is a singular, mesmerizing occasion. It is a great story told. The child, especially, is transported. Here is indeed the discovery of wonder and delight in words. For the child it is an epiphany, a first fulfillment of the imagination. At once and forever nothing will be as it was.

It seems to me that I am that child. I too have had the profound experience of discovering the power of language and literature, first in the oral tradition, then in writing. My father would begin a story with the Kiowa word *Akeah-de*, "They were camping," an ancient verbal formula that reflects the nomadism of the culture and is likely thousands of years old. I was fascinated by the Kiowa stories, and I begged my father to tell them to me over and over again until they were fixed in my mind. I have lived with them for many years and they remain a foundation of my creative expression.

Story is the marrow of literature. The story does not end with the last word. It goes on in the silence of the mind, in that region in which exists the unknown, the mysterious, and that origin of the word in which all words are contained. I profess the conviction that there is only one story, but there are many stories in the one. Literature can be likened to a rolling wheel of language. It reinvents itself with every telling of the story, and in its timeless procession it has neither beginning nor end.

A poem is a moral statement concerning the human condition, composed in verse. It is a moral statement in that it involves judgment and choice. The poet judges the validity of his subject and chooses what he considers the appropriate vehicle of its expression. The judgment is an ethical procedure, as is the reader's (listener's) obligation to judge the poet's judgment. In a real sense the human condition is the universal subject of literature; arguably there is no other. Verse is measure. The basic difference between poetry and prose is that poetry is composed of predetermined measures, iambic pentameter, for example.

The poem, as such, does not exist in Native American oral tradition, for the verbal equivalent is not composed in English poetic measure. Rather, there is song and such verbal variants as oratory, spells, chants, prayers, etc., all informed with poetic or lyrical undercurrents.

In my early career as a poet I wrote out of the oral tradition, making use of the character of Native American expression that I acquired as a birthright and by way of having grown up on Indian reservations in the Southwest, specifically the Navajo, Apache, and Pueblo.

In 1959 I was awarded a Stegner Creative Writing Fellowship at Stanford University, where I studied under the direction of the distinguished poet and critic Yvor Winters, who instructed me in the history of the lyric poem in English. Winters was my true friend, and he influenced my life as a writer in ways that I continue to discover. I am profoundly in his debt.

In my time I have seen many things, and I have traveled widely over the earth. My writing is supported by considerable experience. In Arizona I have seen the Navajo *Yeibichai* and heard the haunting chants of the mountain gods. In Moscow I have seen numerous commuters reading books of poetry on the Metro, and I have attended poetry readings to standing-room-only crowds in large arenas. In Siberia I have heard the Khanty songs of the bear ceremony. And in London I have heard the words of Shakespeare and Ben Johnson. I can only hope that there are soft echoes of these voices in my work. It would be a grateful satisfaction.

At Stanford I experimented with different forms of poetic composition. During my tenure there I received a Guggenheim Fellowship and spent a year on leave in Amherst, Massachusetts, where I read Emily Dickinson in manuscript. She wrote in intricate patterns and rhyme schemes, and she described brilliantly the landscape in which lived her whole life. I learned from her something about the spirit of place.

My friend and predecessor at Stanford, Thom Gunn, tried his hand with syllabic poems, poems measured solely by the number of syllables in each line; I too wrote in syllabics. The 5-7-5 syllabic form basic to haiku is one that informs the section of this collection entitled "A Century of Impressions."

The title poem, "The Death of Sitting Bear," is the memorial to a Kiowa kinsman of extraordinary stature as a warrior and a chief. He inspired fear, wonder, and admiration in large measure, and his death was a self-orchestrated act of extreme bravery, loyalty, and the determination to be free. I feel his presence close by in my blood and imagination, and I sing him an honor song.

Under the title of my poem "Prairie Hymn," the final poem in this collection, is a concise formula from the Chippewa oral tradition:

As my eyes search the prairie
I feel the summer in the spring.

These few words, in the precision, perception, and beauty they express, seem to me to embody the essence of poetry. When I was a boy, waking to the pristine sunrise and seeing the bright land rolling away to the horizon, the seed of poetry was invested in me. I felt the summer in the spring.

N. Scott Momaday

I

Dypaloh. There was a house made of dawn. It was made of pollen and of rain, and the land was very old and everlasting. There were many colors on the hills, and the plain was bright with different-colored clays and sands. Red and blue and spotted horses grazed in the plain, and there was a dark wilderness on the mountains beyond. The land was still and strong. It was beautiful all around.

From *HOUSE MADE OF DAWN*

BEQUEST

Oh, my holy and unholy thoughts
Will lie scattered on these pages.
They will do to make a modest book,
Not something for the ages,
But leavings for a lonely child, perhaps,
Or for an old man dreaming.

IN THE FOREST

For my brother, Yuri Vaella

Oh my brother, I hear your footsteps
In the forest. They are strong and even;
They sound the rhythm of your great heart.
You go among the tracks of the bear.
Always the bear will guide you.
You will come to an open space among the trees,
And there you will dance. You will sing the songs
Of the elders, those who have made sacred the earth.
I hear your footsteps and your songs.
Oh my brother, I will dance with you.
Together we will celebrate our bear being.
We will keep alive the holy fires.
Aiyee!

A SIBERIAN HUNTER, REMEMBRANCE

In taiga I have gone a solemn way.
A Nenets man I found. He had me say
His name, Yuri Vaella, hunter and friend.
His heart is one with mine beyond his end.

TO THE FARTHER CAMPS

In the making of my song
There is a crystal wind
And the burnished dark of dusk
There is the memory of elders dancing
In firelight at Two Meadows
Where the reeds bend eastward
I sing, and there is elation in it
And laughter like the play of spinning leaves
I sing, and I am gone from sorrow
To the farther camps

A DARKNESS COMES

And I have seen the raging of the skies,
The beating of fields in the raucous night,
And waited for the searing dawn and light,
The soaring sun, the swollen earth that dries.
The rutted roads run away to nowhere.
The mind is hardened and the will is lost.
I wish for something in between. And mostly
The wind burns my wishes on the air.
Old men and women gather at the graves
Of pioneers, and broken windmills mark
Distances of despair and, scattered, stark,
The bones of cattle and encrusted staves.

I look across the plain. The weather hums
At dusk. I stiffen, and a darkness comes.

A HERO'S BURIAL

The hours are at hand, the scene is set;
   In readiness the grave.
The dignitaries on the lawn are met
   In solemn stance, and brave.

The hero is interred beneath the flag
   With stark facility.
And now the stately interval will lag
   Into eternity.

Rifles are fired as one, a bugle blown.
   The scent of glory weaves
Among the final notes. And left alone,
   The mound and drifting leaves.

THE KIOWA NO-FACE DOLL

Kiowa Boarding School, Anadarko

They see how you hold your doll
With love and desperation.
Are they to imagine expression
On the bare, impenetrable mask?
There is nothing to reflect
The face of a child, glad or sad,
Who see upon this sere surface
Anonymity only, a random
Fetish of precise uniformity.
For those who brought you here,
You are the image of your doll.
For those who relegated you
To military sameness, you bear
The visage of a faceless race.

A SLOVEN

A sloven entered the parade,
Was out of step and wanted aid
To fashion well a bold charade.

"I am the Emperor Norton."
His cry was heard by everyone,
From Candlestick to Tiburon.

None questioned his high majesty
Nor did gainsay his sovereignty.
His subjects set his spirit free.

The sloven tarried and held sway
Until at last he passed away
And into legend by the bay.

ALASKAN GAMES

A young fox scampers
At the near wall of a pine wood,
Just full of himself.
A raven comes at dusk to play
Hide-and-seek.

She rides on runners
Into the sheer, glistening wind.
The dogs are joyful,
The sky blushes above snowfields,
And she laughs.

The mountain appears,
Silver and pink in the dawn.
The tracks of a lynx
Are drawn straight on the blue slope,
A long slant.

A MODEST BOAST (TOAST)

My mind is sharpened by this sip of mead,
Philosophers attend my wit indeed;
Do not encourage me; there is no need.

A NOTE ON ANIMALS

Do elephants quest? I have seen them lumbering with purpose. Young foxes are so bold as to tease large predatory birds. Ravens watch. Penguins are poker-faced comedians, the Little Tramps of the polar ice. North of Greenland's dog equator, the dogs are alert even as they sleep. Teddy bears are cute and cuddly. Real bears are humiliated. Horses are majestic; the head of a blooded horse is among the most noble images in the world. Within every tropical bush the promise of an iguana. The buffalo is the animal representation of the sun. The nature of whales is godlike. Of all creatures the mosquito is the most irritating and the least necessary. Cats are more dangerous and less intelligent than they appear. Dogs are less dangerous and more intelligent than they appear. The pedigree of dogs is distinguished; all dogs are descended from wolves. Wolves are superior and misunderstood. Snakes are the wise keepers of the underworld. The less said about marmots the better. Man is the most arrogant of the apes.

AGO

My children, when they were very young,
Played in a great landscape, windy and wild,
Near "the place of the bridge" on the Rio Puerco.
In the middle distance were gullies and dunes,
And a train moved slowly eastward
As if stitching patches of color to the earth.
Rabbits ran from the brown and yellow brush.
My children knew the goodness of that place.
Now when I go by, they are there. Something
Of their delight remains among the rocks,
Tsegi, the place of origin. Their laughter slips
On the ripples of sand, and I look after them.

DIVISION

There is a depth of darkness
In the wild country, days of evening
And the silence of the moon.
I have crept upon the bare ground
Where animals have left their tracks,
And faint cries carry on the summits,
Or sink to silence in the muffled leaves.
Here is the world of wolves and bears
And of old, instinctive being,
So noble and indifferent as to be remote
To human knowing. The scales upon which
We seek a balance measure only a divide.

THE NIGHT SKY AT COPPERMINE

At Coppermine we landed in order to take on fuel. We
had come down from Holman Island and were on our
way to Yellowknife. It was the middle of the night. The
plane seated ten or twelve passengers, as I recall, but there
were only five on board. We had been buffeted about in
the wind and snow, and I was feeling the effects. I did
not feel like moving from my seat, but at the same time I
thought that a blast of cold fresh air might do me good,
and I could at least stretch my legs. When I came to the
door, the wind was rushing in with such force that I was
nearly knocked backward. I braced myself and struggled
out on the stairway. Then my breath caught in my throat.
The Northern Lights were hanging, roiling, whipping
on the sky, descending squarely upon me. The shock of
this magnificent light show was greater than that of the
icy wind, and I was stunned again. But nothing could
distract me from what I was seeing: the snowy night sky
unraveling into great ribbons of dancing color. I had seen
the Northern Lights before, but they were never like these.
It was an event of great spiritual moment, such as children
know in their wonder and innocence. It was Christmas in
the universe.

SONG FRAGMENTS

1 (Lullaby)

In the crook of my arm, place your head there,
And I shall sing you a song of white bread and rye.
And if you care not for my bread lullaby,
I shall hum you the way to Northampton Fair.

2 (Blues)

Memphis Mister, play that horn for me.
Play it slow, play a down-and-out melody.
My woman done left me, left me high and dry.
My baby done left me. Gonna lay me down and die.

3 (Folk)

Hang him high, Sheriff Garrett;
Don't let the Kid go free.
Hang him high, Sheriff Garrett,
Hang him from a white oak tree.

4 (Country)

Give me a honky-tonk girl,
Give me a honky-tonk girl.
Give me a girl whose skirts do swirl.
Step to the front and step to the rear.
Give me a hot wing and a bottle of beer.

FOR WALLACE STEVENS

Yes, I know that time.
Evening is the afternoon,
Snow is incessant.
And blackbirds sit in the limbs.

Do you know *this* time?
Magpies range in the meadows,
And antelope graze
In foothills of the mountains.

When the blackbird flies
There is a deep emptiness
In which presence was,
In which nameless nothing is.

When the magpie flies
There is a bright arrogance
Of four colors, a
Flag for holy clowns, God's own.

THE WOMAN LOOKING IN

Near the Taganka Theatre she stands
At a window, shaping talk with her hands,
Wearing a fur-trimmed coat, a white fur hat
And boots. The photograph is bare and flat:
The woman, window, wall and winter fixed
In time, in drab where cold and soot are mixed.
And yet there is a luster on the plane,
As specters of the Northern Lights remain.
I imagine the woman is resolved
To tell a fate in which I am involved.
I've seen the tragedy performed next door
And seen the ghost that wanders Elsinore.
Perhaps the woman sees beyond the glass
A spirit schooled in semblance and morass.
Or is she poor Ophelia gone insane
And peering through the frosted windowpane?
The lens has opened on the dismal air,
And nothing that the woman sees is there.

TRANSPARENCY

I make you this gift with love,
An expression of my spirit
In clean strokes and bright colors.
Seen for the composition it is,
A road curves out to an edge of time,
There is the burn of the setting sun
And twisted brads in the foreground.

Beneath these pigments an abstraction:
Beheld in its deeper meaning,
In the pure aspect of imagining,
There is a muted evening looming
In the ocher of orchards and autumn fields,
And in the lambent flurry of leaves,
You, intrinsic on the plane of desire.

SPECTRE

How faint her humble form
Suspended there among the stars.
She wears the mantle of a mendicant,
Blue or black and meager against the cold.
At her throat the winding of a shroud
Extends the pallor of her face
Into the water hue of her hair.
She bears no expression,
But a silence pulses at her lips
Like lost whispers of the Magdalen.
And she stands in the glitter of God,
Against disclosure and the chill of heaven.

THE GREAT FILLMORE STREET BUFFALO DRIVE

Insinuate the sun through fog
upon Pacific Heights, upon the man on horseback,
upon the herd ascending. *There* is color and clamor.

And there he waves them down,
those great humpbacked animals,
until their wild grace gone
they lumber and lunge
and blood blisters at their teeth
and their hooves score the street—
and among boulders they settle on the sea.

He looks after them, twisted round upon his sorrow,
the drape of his flag now full and formal,
ceremonial.

One bull, animal representation of the sun,
he dreams back from the brink
to the green refuge of his hunter's heart.
It grazes near a canyon wall,
along a ribbon of light, among redbud trees,
eventually into shadow.

Then the hold of his eyes is broken;
on the farther rim the grasses flicker and blur,
a hawk brushes rain across the dusk,
meadows recede into mountains, and here and there
are moons like salmonberries
upon the glacial face of the sky.

THE SNOW MARE

In my dream, a blue mare loping,
Pewter on a porcelain field, away.
There are bursts of soft commotion
Where her hooves drive in the drifts,
And as dusk ebbs on the plane of night,
She shears the web of winter,
And on the far, blind side
She is no more. I behold nothing,
Wherein the mare dissolves in memory,
Beyond the burden of being.

THE BONE STRIKERS

They stand grim in the distance,
Brandishing the bones with which
They strike. They are counted on
Though they are poor and wretched

In their wounds. Yet they are sung
Among the camps, and their shields
Are regarded with fear and wonder.
How plain is their regalia! How rude

Their savage style! They are chosen,
And in the choice there is severance
And sorrow. In near time they will go
And roam the darkness, having gone.

YAHWEH TO URSET

I pray that you are kept safe throughout this day, that you live as wholly as you can, that you see things that you have not seen before and that more of them are beautiful than not, more of them delightful than not. I pray that you hold easily in your hands the balance of the earth and sky, that you laugh and cry, know freedom and restraint, some joy and some sorrow, pleasure and pain, much of life and a little of death. I pray that you are grateful for the gift of your being, and I pray that you celebrate your life in the proper way, with grace and humility, wonder and contentment, in the strong, deep current of your spirit's voice. I pray that you are happily in love in the dawn and that you are more deeply in love in the dusk.

THE ESSENCE OF BELONGING

Consider the shiver of the mirrored moon:
You appear in the shredded light,
A figure fixed in approach, suspended.

Like Nolde's *Sternenwandler* you stand
Mysterious among the stars. You persist,
And a clean wind measures your persistence.

Along a cleavage in space the day becomes,
And you conspire in the invention of belonging,
Radiant, jealously imagined, estranged from time,

And to the crowded habitation of the mind
You bring a solitude, a mere and sensual silence
In which the essence of belonging belongs.

TO AN AGED BEAR

Hold hard this infirmity.
It defines you. You are old.

Now fix yourself in summer,
In thickets of ripe berries,

And venture toward the ridge
Where you were born. Await there

The setting sun. Be alive
To that old conflagration

One more time. Mortality
Is your shadow and your shade.

Translate yourself to spirit;
Be present on your journey.

Keep to the trees and waters.
Be the singing of the soil.

THE BEAR

What ruse of vision
escarping the wall of leaves,
  rending incision
into countless surfaces,

  would cull and color
his somnolence, whose old age
  has outworn valor,
all but the fact of courage?

  Seen, he does not come,
Move, but seems forever there,
  Dimensionless, dumb,
In the windless noon's hot glare.

  More scarred than others
These years since the trap maimed him,
  Pain slants his withers,
drawing up the crooked limb.

  Then he is gone, whole,
Without urgency, from sight,
  As buzzards control,
Imperceptibly, their flight.

A BENIGN SELF-PORTRAIT

A mirror will suffice, no doubt.
The high furrowed forehead,
The heavy-lidded Asian eyes,
The long-lobed Indian ears.
Brown skin beginning to spot,
Of an age to bore and be bored.
I turn away, knowing too well
My face, my expression
For all seasons, my half smile.

Birds flit about the feeder,
The dog days wane, and I
Observe the jitters of leaves
And the pallor of the ice-blue beyond.
I read to find inspiration. I write
To restore candor to the mind.
There are raindrops on the window,
And a peregrine wind gusts on the grass.
I think of my old red flannel shirt,
The one I threw away in July.
I would like to pat the warm belly of a
Beagle or the hand of a handsome woman.
I look ahead to cheese and wine,
And a bit of Bach, perhaps,
Or Schumann on the bow of Yo-Yo Ma.

I see the mountains as I saw them
When my heart was young.

But were they not a deeper blue,
Shimmering under the fluency of skies
Radiant with crystal light? Across the way
The yellow land lies out, and standing stones
Form distant islands in the field of time.
There is a stillness on this perfect world,
And I am content to settle in its hold.
I turn inward on a wall of books.
They are old friends, even those that
Have dislodged my dreams. One by one
They have shaped the thing I am.

These are the days that swarm
Into the shadows of legend. I ponder.
And when the image on the glass
Is refracted into the prisms of the past
I shall remember: my parents speaking
Quietly in a warm familiar room, and
I bend to redeem an errant, broken doll.
My little daughter, her eyes brimming
With love, beholds the ember of my soul.
There is the rattle of a teacup, and
At the window and among the vines,
The whir of a hummingbird's wings.
In the blue evening, in another room,
There is the faint laughter of ghosts,
And in a tarnished silver frame, the
likeness of a boy who bears my name.

PRAYER FOR WORDS

My voice restore for me.
        —NAVAJO

Here is the wind bending the reeds westward,
The patchwork of morning on gray moraine:

Had I words I could tell of origin,
Of God's hands bloody with birth at first light,
Of my thin squeals in the heat of his breath,
Of the taste of being, the bitterness,
And scents of camas root and chokecherries.

And, God, if my mute heart expresses me,
I am the rolling thunder and the bursts
Of torrents upon rock, the whispering
Of old leaves, the silence of deep canyons.
I am the rattle of mortality.

I could tell of the splintered sun. I could
Articulate the night sky, had I words.

ON THE CAUSE OF A HOMELY DEATH

Even the ashes are instilled
In dust. Imagine it was age
And worthy destiny fulfilled,
Not fear, not loneliness, not rage.

THE BLIND ASTROLOGERS

Now, at evening, we hear them.
They sheer and shuffle, cracking
Branches and heaving the air.
Always shyly they appear.

In radiance they take shape
Faintly, their great heads hung low
On arcs of age, their dull eyes
Compassing the murky moon.

They sway and impress the earth
With claws. They incise the ice.
Stars of the first magnitude
Pulse the making of their dance.

They ascend the ancient bridge
And lay fishes in our way,
So to feed us and our dogs.
Along the green slant southward

The blind astrologers blaze
The long traces of our quest.
They lead us, dead reckoning
By the suns they cannot see.

We regard them with wonder,
Fear, and sorrow. They mutter
And cry with voices like ours;
They mime a human anguish.

When they take their leave they fade
Through planes and prisms of rain
Into the drifts of story,
Into calendars and names.

THE PURSUIT OF MAN BY GOD

Do you not know me?
I AM that I AM. I am
The guise I affect
In holy art and scripture.

But I am also
A tempest of dark colors,
Primal predator,
Jealous of my Creation.

You will appease me
For I am close on your heels.
In humility,
In futility your flight.

Hear the wind raging
In my hot, impending breath.
In merciful fury
I will take fast hold of you.

REVENANT

You are the dark shape I find
On nights of the spilling moon,
Pale in the pool of heaven.
You are spirit, you are that
Which summons me and confirms
My passage. You know my name.
Your ritual dance remarks
The crooked way between me
And the very thing you are:
Mask, essence, and revenant.
You are, as you ever were,
The energy that sustains
My mere despair. And always
You are the dark shape I find.

DEATH COMES FOR BEOWULF

Oh, man, this is *wyrd*. You shine
In beaten gold and glory. You are
Summoned, and you come without question.
The Danes know of you. Indeed, who does not?
Among your trappings, fame and fearlessness,
The carriage of a conqueror, a Geat, a god.
One by one inhuman beings turn to gore
At your hurtful hands.

But you too grow old, even as do those
Whose lives you have saved and handed back—
To what avail? All of life is but the flutter of wings
Barely trembling on the walls of the high hall.
You are not demented in your age. You are Beowulf.
And for the last time you are summoned.
Then there is glory without triumph, a worthy
Equality in death.

A black wind whirls on the smoldering pyre,
And much is ended. *Heofon rece swealg.*

THE MYTHIC HARPOON

In groves of eucalyptus
We looked into the channel
Where gray whales rode in passage,
Their flukes flagging errant gulls
And tunneling drifting waves.
And they sounded into depths
As dark as death, as unknown.
Always they held us in thrall.
Instinctively we dreamt them,
And our dream was driven home,
Deep into the cresting curve,
A quick line taut in the mind,
The mind reeling out of mind,
Tethered to the tumult there.

BEFORE AN OLD PAINTING OF THE CRUCIFIXION

I ponder how He died, despairing once.
I've heard the cry subside in vacant skies,
In clearings where no other was. Despair,
Which in the vibrant wake of utterance,
Resides in desolate calm, preoccupies.
Though it is still. There is no solace there.

That calm inhabits wilderness, the sea,
And where no peace inheres but solitude;
Near death it most impends. It was for Him,
Absurd and public in His agony,
Inscrutably itself, nor misconstrued,
Nor metaphrased in art or pseudonym:

A vague contagion. Old, the mural fades . . .
Reminded of the fainter sea I scanned,
I recollect: How mute in constancy!
I could not leave the wall of palisades
Till cormorants returned my eyes on land.
The mural but implies eternity.

Not death, but silence after death is change.
Judean hills, the endless afternoon,
The farther groves and arbors seasonless
But fix the mind within the moment's range.

Where evening would obscure our sorrow soon,
There shines too much a sterile loveliness.

No imprecisions of commingled shade,
No shimmering deceptions of the sun.
Herein no semblances remark the cold
Unhindered swell of time, for time is stayed.
The Passion wanes into oblivion.
And time and timelessness confuse, I'm told.

These centuries removed from either fact
Have lain upon the critical expanse
And been of little consequence. The void
Is calendared in stone; the human act,
Outrageous, is in vain. The hours advance
Like flecks of foam borne landward and destroyed.

A SILENCE LIKE FROST

A silence like frost hovers here.
I look for the promise of being,
But only the bare presence of death appears.
I think of who I am and do not know.
The God in whom I scarcely believe
Is smug with me, tendering forgiveness,
But as much as I, he is culpable.
Here in these words is no silence broken,
But silence lays a rime upon them,
And, burdened with cold, they die away.

On the wall across from my window
A scarlet leaf spins slowly down,
Touching here and there those that cling
To the dark tangle of their waning life.
It catches the bare edges of light
And rocks into the drift and scatter below.

ANGLE OF GEESE

How shall we adorn
Recognition with our speech?—
  Now the dead firstborn
Will lag in the wake of words.

  Custom intervenes;
We are civil, something more.
  More than language means
The mute presence mulls and marks.

  Almost of a mind
We take measure of the loss;
  I am slow to find
The mere margin of repose.

  And one November
It was longer in the watch,
  As if forever,
Of the huge ancestral goose.

  So much symmetry!—
Like the pale angle of time
  And eternity—
The great shape labored and fell.

  Quit of hope and hurt,
It held a motionless gaze
  Wide of time, alert,
On the dark, distant flurry.

BIRDSONG

Her voice was ever alive.
When first I heard it
I thought it was birdsong.
Even now her words trip
And ripple on the air. There is
A warbler in the meadow.

SHADE

You are present in the past
And appear in memory,
A braid of smoke, a vapor,
And silence is your substance.
You are nothing. Yet you are.
You wend along the long way
To a perfect destiny
On a whisper of the wind.

ON THE NEVA

He waits, who describes rainbows.
Then more than the morning wind
Strums the beaded string.
He sets himself, sturdy on the plane of ice.
Nearly numb, his hands tease and turn
The frantic shadow into the circle below him
And suddenly heave it into sight,
And when it strikes the air
It freezes instantly and becomes iridescent,
And traces a perfect arc across
The soft and smoking sun.

THE WHALE IN AMBER

A broken beach lies there beyond
the rutted road. The wood
inclines landward to the sky.
Now is the quick quality
of regenerated blood,
the present that does not die.

To be is to tread in time
and place. Always are the dead
beyond our ambitious reach.
They invoke their perfect prime
to sanction this narrow stead
and conjoin us each to each.

Above, the embers of time,
barren in the ashen void,
are strewn in random litter.
Stasis humbles the sublime.
Rule and motion are destroyed
in the stark glacial glitter.

The platter eye of the whale
Holds the span. The great wayward
beast would churn the lunar light
and arc the undulant glow,
the sea its dark amber, hard
about it, in timeless night.

THE DRAGON OF SAINT-BERTRAND-DE-COMMINGES

The cathedral above the plain describes
The faith of a medieval town, and yet
Informs three ages of architecture.
Roman remains of gate and garrison

Stand to the blue rise of the Pyrenees
And reflect the glory of far conquest.
Now pastoral the military ruin;
The haze of the valley is sweet-scented.

From the cloister the Haute-Garonne lies out
In a surround of lavender and green.
High up the ghosts of artisans arrange
The facets of stained glass into story.

And in a dark recess the dragon hangs.
In its grotesque and knobbed and leather length
It bears witness to the veiled truth of myth:
Monsters and men once flourished under God,

And children of the mountains crept herein
To tremble in the presence of the fact.
The cave of the Cathedral is a lair,
And there, in faith, to see is to believe.

NOUS AVONS VU LA MER

We have been lovers,
you and I.
We have been alive
in the clear mornings of Genesis;
in the afternoons,
among the prisms of the air,
our hands have shaped perfect silences.
We have seen the sea;
wonder is well known to us.

A CHRONICLE

Now they are gone who told me what I know,
And I shall follow though my pace be slow.
God grant me tenure and a time to go.

BEFORE AND AFTER

In the window
The dim rear view
Of a naked woman,
And beyond her a man
Transparent as the rain,
Standing at an easel
And stroking color
To a canvas plane.
Her nape and shoulders
Shimmer in soft light;
A symmetry flares from
The dimple of her spine.
The artist, concentrated,
Sees what is before him,
The poet sees what is not.
It is an equitable equation.

THE THEFT OF IDENTITY

They say my footprints are those of a bear.
Yes, it is true. I crave the mountain air
And find retirement in a lofty lair.
Believe it or not; I really don't care.

Hey ho yah,
Hey ho yah,
Humph!

A COUPLET IN TONGUES

She spoke a language known only to God.
God gave a nod. Nothing to God is odd.

DICTUM

If language is the instrument of thought
And one relies on reason as one ought,
Then words hold surely what is seen and sought.

NEED

A grave mythology indeed,
The story of the widow's need,
The story of the landlord's greed.

JFK

We wept and could not put our grief aside
And knew it was our innocence that died.

SONG OF LONGING

Will you come to me now
You must know that in the firelight
I wait for you with longing
You are there in the range
   Of my desire
Will you come to me now
Thee white moon shines on the cornfields
Evening falls among the melon rows
The orange sun sets on the mountains
The river runs sparkling on blue stones
   And the long reeds bend and sway
I will welcome you with sweetgrass and sage
Will you come to me now
I sing in my heart of your coming
I sing in my soul of your coming

STONES

There are things of strange aspect in the world, things that you come upon without expectation, and they are the more meaningful for that. One day, on an Easter Sunday, I was walking in the foothills of the Pamir Mountains in Central Asia. It was a brilliant morning, full of crystal clear air in a green and lavender landscape that intensified the shadows of clouds sailing across the sun. I found myself in a dry wash, a narrow depression in which water must have run after hard rains. There were stones about, stones of various colors and shapes, such as you see in the beds of mountain streams. Then, remarkably, I saw at my feet three white stones. They were exactly alike, and they were precisely the size and shape of hens' eggs. After nearly half a century I have not forgotten them. They were, I believe, the gifts of the goddess Eostre, of whom I knew nothing at the time. Such stones contain an ancient story of survival and renewal. The story is told from year to year, and it becomes more nearly complete with each telling.

POEM AFTER LUNCH

Cheeses, fruit, exotic tea,
A simple repast, gardenside,
Under a yellow umbrella.
Bright sampler of the afternoon.
Not only that. I tasted of
That entity that was the two
Of us, that composition
Of conjoined being
In the clarity of autumn.

APPROACH

It will approach without your consent
It will stand before you without cheer
  or malice
It will not be without meaning
But it will mean without your understanding
It will reveal nothing without
But without caprice or ambiguity
It will reveal the cold reality within

ENGLISH, THE LANGUAGE

It is so much in vogue,
There are so many words.

Words, those conceptual symbols,
Are used to build poems

And to guide airplanes into Calcutta.
We must respect them; they are sacred.

It is said that words, once spoken,
Remain in the air forever. I hope so,

Although I would prefer silence
To many utterances I have heard

Or made indeed. Let us not harvest
All the words floating in the air. Instead,

Let us hear in our most receptive minds
The words of Shakespeare and Winnie the Pooh.

A STORY OF LIGHT

When the leaves turn
And the light of the forest deepens,
I will remember a thousand words between us.
Those that enclosed us, as in the pattern
Of shadows that shiver with the turning leaves,
Recount a story that was told about us by those
Who told stories in the caves. We danced
To the music of the words. On our tongues
Were shaped the names of our original being.
This is what the storyteller said: The leaves turn,
And in the light that emanates from the leaves
There is enchantment. There is wonder.

THIS TRAIN

Who will ride this train,
Moving on tracks of time?
Who will ride this train?
Who will hear the wheels
Rolling, metal on metal, grinding
Distance away toward the sea?

This train will stitch patches of color
To the fields. This train will make
A seam along the taiga,
And rivers will reflect its passing.
There will be the middle of nowhere.
Who will ride this train?

This train will sever the nights and days,
Trailing sound through random towns,
And defined in the vague lights of forgotten
Outposts. This train will run
To some destiny at the end of the road.
Who will ride this train?

WAR CHRONICLE

Memorial Day, 2010

There came the beast, rapacious and obscene.
There came hysteria. We watched the sky
Implode, the steep flight of dark angels, keen
And shrill, like meteors before they die.

And ragged children of the ruins roved
In roiling smoke and scatter of debris.
In loss and lunacy so were they moved
To balance madness and mere sanity.

Let sunlight gather in their hollow hands,
And solace be the harvest of their fears,
Purchased with pain, dry seeds in sterile sands,
Until from ashen night the dawn appears.

THE RIDER OF TWO GRAY HILLS

To the Mountain of Thunder I ride
My horse is the slithering wind
In his tracks will blessings follow

In the place of moonlit waters
I will slake my thirst and sleep
In the dawn I will make my prayer
and ride on

There will be wonders about me
Bright lightning on obsidian skies
Rain and rainbows shining
Grasses shivering

There will be laughter in my heart
The Holy Ones will look out for me

VISITATION AT AMHERST

She must have mused for centuries.
Celestial buttons at her eyes,
Until no mould could crust her soul,
Whirling in the wind of words.

FIRE

Here now
the smoldering minds of men
who tell the stories of themselves
whose imagination flares in the void
They wage the silent wars
burning in conflagrations of thought
and the cinders of the soul
Here now
the thrust and parry of words
in the chronic quarrel with God
the words like sparks
notions like tinder
and reason the whipping of the wind

FIRST POEM

Light edging spears of grass,
Water running through time.
The moon in mist,
Words bleeding.

MEDITATION ON WILDERNESS

In the evening's orange and umber light,
There come vagrant ducks skidding on the pond.
Together they veer inward to the reeds.
The forest—aspen, oak, and pine—recedes,
And the sky is smudged on the ridge beyond.
There is more in my soul than in my sight.

I would move to the other side of sound;
I would be among the bears, keeping still,
Not watching, waiting instead. I would dream,
And in that old bewilderment would seem
Whole in a beyond of dreams, primal will
Drawn to the center of this dark surround.

The sacred here emerges and abides.
The day burns down, the hours dissolve in time;
The bears parade the deeper continent
As silences pervade the firmament,
And wind wavers on the radiant rime.
Here is the house where wilderness resides.

OLGA

She was a woman of exceptional intelligence and grace. In her native Russia she had earned a most enviable reputation as a linguist and lexicographer. As a girl in the Russian Revolution she suffered severe hardship, and yet she saw to the survival of two young siblings. She had stories to tell. By sheer will she rose to a high position in the Moscow State University. There we met in 1974, behind the Iron Curtain and in the heat of the Cold War. We became fast friends almost at once. She was several decades older than I, but she had kept two remarkable things throughout her life, in spite of the hard times she had endured, a keen sense of humor and a childlike delight in the world. She loved to have people around her, and she seemed to find every one of them interesting. Once we attended a luncheon at which there were a number of high-ranking officials and traditional bureaucrats. There were toasts and preliminary speeches, all of which took a long time. Then the main speaker was introduced, and I whispered to my companion in a sympathetic tone, "I suppose he will speak at great length." Her eyes sparkled and she replied, "Oh, I hope so!?"

THE GALLERIES

Do you sense them there, the ones
Who invented art, who saw
That we might see? They linger
Now within these galleries,
Mute, marginal in their minds,
And surpassing in their touch.

What masterpieces they wrought,
Images that leapt through time,
Engulfed in the perfect night
Of millennia and cold,
Skeletal stillness, pending,
Closer than the walls around.

How did they reckon future,
Indeed immortality?
The primal forms they imaged
Yet proceed from some beyond.
They remain, undivided
From the dead and vital hand.

REMEMBERING MILOSZ AND "ESSE"

She got out at Raspail. I was left behind with the immensity of existing things. A sponge, suffering because it cannot saturate itself; a river, suffering because reflections of clouds and trees are not clouds and trees.

—CZESLAW MILOSZ, "ESSE"

A season of breeze-borne light,
And, in your phrase, "the immensity of existing things,"
   Enclosed us there.
Among listeners you read almost in confidence,
Almost in the apology of creation,
   And the chord of conscience.
What was it that "Esse" meant to you?
Your voice was grave, in the timbre of loss.
You recited in the measure of the heart's broken pulse.
I wanted to know you, to have known you
For many years
   In the immensity of existing things.
Afterwards you returned to yourself;
You were definitively Milosz, gracious and at ease,
An old man of an old Europe, a gentleman
Of languages. You attempted to name the world,
And in precise syllables you succeeded.
   Outside, among the elder trees
And beside the grassy banks of a slow, transparent stream,
You seemed to contemplate an unforgiving history,
and the difference between clouds and their reflection.

DEATH SONG

In the crescent formed
They are fearful in their stance,
  Their sashes impaled,
The arrows throb to the song:
  The sun and the moon
Will live forever, but we
  Kaitsenko die.
And each soldier holds his place
  And the field is won
Or given up to the dead.
  Away in the camps
There is bright water running
  Between banks of reeds
And prairie turnips. The drone
  Of bees a music
On sagebrush and bluebonnets,
  Women and children
Frolic among butterflies,
  And hawks in the sky
Circle and sail on the wind.
  On the trail of time
It is a good day to die.

DICHOS

Neither do I believe in time. Time is the red rock and the blue cloud floating above Oljeto.

My horse knows the meeting place of the earth and sky. Rain darkens his flanks. A snake, and the whites of his eyes.

The long arc of the red mesa; it has to be seen at sunrise, when fire informs it from within.

So, the Pedernal is yours. The Valle Grande is mine. We must trade, back and forth, in good relation to each other.

There was malice in the eyes of the eagle, wasn't there?

Only in the time of roasting is the chili darker than pine needles, and turquoise deeper than the sky.

I dreamed that all the prisms of the air converged on the plaza at Abiquiu.

The patio gate is old. In my memory the woman is old, discerning, not quite humble, almost arrogant, certainly no one but herself. She is a great artist. I am honored.

A WITNESS TO CREATION

If you could have that one day back, the one that you have kept a secret in your soul, what day would it be?

What? One among the many? Well, let me make you this offering:

It would be the day on which I stood on the rim of Monument Valley and beheld those ineffable monoliths for the first time. I was young, you see, like a fledgling who leaves the nest and flies out over the earth. I saw beyond time, into timelessness. It was the first and holiest of all days. On such a day—on *that* original day—did the First Man behold the First World. It filled him with wonder and humility. Then and there, looking for one enchanted moment into eternity, I was the First Man. I was present at Creation.

SOBREMESA

Did you chip the calf, Alfredo?
Sí, I chipped the calf, Jose.
Did you ride with your knees, Alfredo?
With my knees and heart, Jose.
Did your horse sling his head, Alfredo?
Sí, his head was slung low, Jose.
Did he see into the calf's eyes, Alfredo?
Sí, he saw into the eyes, Jose.
What did he see there Alfredo?
Nada. There was nothing to see, Jose.
You have a fine cutting horse, Alfredo.
Sí, mine is a fine cutting horse, Jose.
Por favor, have one more, Alfredo.
Sí, gracias, one more for the ride, Jose.

APPEARANCES

1

I know
Of certain things:
An advancing glacier.
A stallion on the skyline
At dusk, a snake skin
On a long golden dune.

2

Below
A canyon rim
I saw two horsemen
Singing a riding song.
They knew who they were.
I knew only their knowing.

3

There where
The mountains rise
In the north and the reeds
Bend eastward, I have seen
The edge of a sacred world.
There are the fringes of rain.

4

At dawn
Beyond the buttes
And through fringes of rain,
The sun appears, low in brilliance,
Ranging from the beginning to the end
Of time. There is only prayer to be said.

ARREST

All day under
flailing snow and

there the membrane
of the sky

curdled and gray
beyond a web of limbs

in the cracks of cold

a blackbird holds still
in the center of sight

and I cannot
look away

AN OASIS THERE OF MANY COLORS

It is different now
But in my early childhood
The mouth of Canyon de Chelly—
An oasis there of many colors
And the sounds of *dine bizaad*
And the sizzle of fry bread—
Must have been among
The four or five best places on earth

AFTERIMAGE

Then I passed the open door,
And then the afterimage
Of a presence in the room:
In the instant it regarded me,
And I had been memorized,
Burdened forever by something
In whose sight or sightlessness
I should remain beside myself,
My deepest self without my reach.
Ahead the cold of the corridor
And the afterimage adhering.

THE LISTENER

To one who listens in the cold
Among the black branches
Of trees braced upon the sky,

There are the long voices of wolves
Rising to the tooth of the moon.
Night describes the summits

Until the northern dawn descends,
And in its polar fringes the voices
Of wolves ring into the void.

To one who listens there is dread,
For the darkness of time extends
Beyond light, beyond the call of wolves.

THE FIRST DAY

The fading moon
and the vanguard of the sun

Alchemy

The immensity of mountains
rising black from the underworld
I behold Creation

In this mindless moment I am intensely alive
There is again the birth of my soul
I am who never was

It is the first day

REVISION OF THE PLAINS

1.

In the evening there are partings
In the steadfast grass, whipped by rain.
The sky furrows on the dusk.

Cattle cluster in the distance
And sound the drone of hollow land,
Drift spinning in the wake of wind.

There is no anguish in the heart,
Only the nature to abide
And heed the farther darkening,

The heat rising on the currents
Of air. A mere periphery
Of loss describes the will to be.

The random rifts will not assuage.
The crooked rivulets will run
And run out. Other storms will come.

2.

The moon dissolves in bands of smoke
And there is havoc in the trees.
The old storm spirit is about.

We speak brave words to stay its ire.
"Oh Man-ka-ih, pass over me!
We are a people of the sun!"

3.

The river rises in tumult.
The banks, the color of dried blood,
Run down with mud. Dark debris boils

In eddies. Flashes strike among
The crumpled surfaces of foam
And the night cracks and breaks open.

4.

The earth is bathed in violence.
Then stars appear and disappear,
And there emerges a clear dawn.

An isolated animal,
A bull of the Criollo strain,
Saunters to a wallow and drinks.

Blithely it swings its horns and wades
And kneels into the rainwater,
Gazing the far edge of landscape.

A shadow darts across the way,
Succinct, incisive, and remote:
There is revision of the Plains.

Seasons will not absent the soil
But grind it into pottery—
And monuments the russet bluffs.

No storm can sunder this expanse,
For ever will the calm become
Again the genesis of time.

And ever will the sailing sun,
Strike to the center of the eye,
And singe the stillness and the stone.

A BLOOMING OF APPEARANCES

Around a nucleus of reality
There is the vacancy of clouds.
Nearly opaque the massive forms,
But they are vagrant and beyond.
There is no substance, only show,
A blooming of appearances.
Rain falls in the troughs of oceans,
And light, as through a prism,
Imposes arcs of color
On the unreality of clouds.
One sees them, and they sail
In sterile, steady winds. And there,
In the vague dimension of illusion,
They cast empty shadows on the earth.

SWEETGRASS

I give you sweetgrass
That you may burn it
That smoke may touch you
That smoke may linger about you
The writhing smoke your dancing
The fragrant smoke your spirit
That the medicine smoke of sweetgrass
May welcome me to you

RUSTIC DREAM

We speak of loss
And rue the gain
And think across
The loss again.
Please ponder this,
This dream of mine:
An edifice
Of ancient pine
In which you lie
On eiderdown,
And snowflakes fly
Above the town,
And on the stove
A potion brews.
The senses rove,
The mind construes.

SEVERANCE

One hears the river run,
An occasional rise of wind.
Nothing of the setting sun
Illuminates the wounded mind.

A coalescence of the dead
Will simulate a marching band
And stitch the way with lurid thread
And echo silence out of hand.

In faith one is compelled to be
Complicit in apostasy.

SEASONAL

Large in grandeur, ripening,
the days went burnished down.
Dusk seared the edge of evening
with cold upon the lawn.

Summer had gathered in the trees
and darkness feathered there
on huddled wings and vagrant leaves,
a season broken bare.

A wind flared in the fields
and random rain became
the silver on the air that yields
to bone and porcelain.

The birds took leave across the hills,
no shadow left behind.
A crescive silence falls and fills
the hollows of the mind.

ROUGH RIDER

The horses went round and round,
And there was a music to their going.
Slowly they leaped and
Slowly they floated down.

Counterclockwise,
One followed upon another.
I rode one of the horses years ago,
A black stallion named Johnnycake.

Annie Oakley dead-eyed a roll-your-own from my lips,
And old Bill himself rallied round the canebrake
And shot a buffalo. I held on to the brass pole
And performed a trick or two. Sitting Bull cheered.

ALMOST LOVE

You answer the door laughing;
It is the laughter of welcome.

You take my hand and lead me
As if my hand were a gift.

You make me think I know you,
That I have known you in childhood

And in the winters of war, that
I have lain with you on silver sands

And braided sweetgrass in your hair.
I imagine moonlight on your breasts

And green lightning in your eyes.
It is almost love, almost a story to tell.

ON SPRING IN THE ALEXANDER GARDENS

Flowers have come from Central Asia,
And old people hold their faces to the sun.
There is rejuvenation in the patient heart
And ice breaking in the waterways.
Grandmother, close your eyes and give thanks,
Tomorrow will be time to sweep the streets.

THIS MORNING THE WHIRLING WIND

It was full of angry sound,
It was not, but its fury was visible.
I watched the tumult among the leaves
And thought of needles of the sun,
How they stitched a stillness
Beneath the green blur of havoc.

II

Now as I look back on that long landscape of the Jemez Valley, it seems to me that I have seen much of the world. And I have been glad to see it, glad beyond the telling. But what I see now is this: If I should hear at evening the wagons on the river road and the voices of children playing in the cornfields, or if in the sunrise I should see the long shadows running out to the west and the cliffs flaring up in the light ascending, or if riding out on an afternoon cool with rain I should see in the middle distance the old man Francisco with his flock, standing deep in the colors and patterns of the plain, it would again be all that I could hold in my heart.

From THE NAMES

A CENTURY OF IMPRESSIONS

1.

on the frosted path
the tracks of many children
crisscross in the noon

2.

summer on the hills
poppies bursting in the sun
five colors rampant

3.

a stone outcropping
gray keeper of a green field
ever standing fast

4.

now the rain-swept plain
tomorrow the burning brush
and the weather rolling

5.

I sit holding her
my lady cello trembling
vibrant her long throat

6.

I behold your hands
the instruments of planting
shaping the harvests

7.

again the snowfall
a shroud of billowing lace
the sheer wind muffled

8.

who will love my face
when age has come upon me
the dog by the hearth

9.

another birthday
a wind in the chimney
a metronome ticks

10.

there are those who know
the prisms in the sunrise
the flakes in the air

11.

strolling in the hills
I am mindful of motion
the river wanders

12.

slowly the reeds dance
the wild river slaps its banks
encore of applause

13.

beyond the forest
a pool of eternity
in the sun's saddle

14.

an eagle soaring
the wind a reflecting plane
mirror of passage

15.

a dark hinge of time
eclipse of the burning shield
and shadows crawling

16.
vapor of the sun
a haze on the mountainside
a curtain of smoke

17.
an antelope bounds
a tumult in the long grass
and evanescence

18.
in the photograph
a black and blue horse bolting
outburst of silence

19.
a young girl praying
and a hundred koi darting
an efficacy

20.
the ringing of wires
artificial birds abound
the bells of heaven

21.

wan the smile of cats

although the mice are aware

ominous the guise

22.

the tide appearing

absorbed in the silver sand

again and again

23.

the desert at dawn

the flowering saguaro

the drumming of rain

24.

geese sliding on ice

the whistling of reeds

pond music at dusk

25.

an aged merchant

a placard in the window

everything must go

26.
woman of the night
a hard makeup at the eyes
a porcelain doll

27.
the ballerina
a spiral of leaps and turns
lifesize music box

28.
in the great bahnhof
silver serpents side by side
Paris overnight

29.
an old dream of you
vivid as the autumn moon
dissolved in the dawn

30.
carols of the mind
on the pale magenta sky
the soul emerging

31.

the crow in the tree
a black tyrant making fun
a rabbit dancing

32.

a lone evergreen
a sentinel bearing snow
tells the time of cold

33.

the wind chides the cranes
they stand in the fallow fields
tall and tolerant

34.

a stone for grinding
shaped by the labor of years
and a woman's hand

35.

ruts of wagon wheels
incise the Oregon Trail
graves marked and unmarked

36.

old ghosts of the house
at home in the darkened rooms
thin benign spirits

37.

the land's crystal light
on the colors of canyons
here my pots of paint

38.

in her quiet space
she wrote of evanescence
and quicksilver days

39.

the house wastes away
there was life and laughter here
who shall remember

40.

time keeps the meadows
cattle low by the river
a bunched committee

41.
the plain in moonlight
a luminous patchwork quilt
fireflies stitch the sky

42.
a sudden downpour
a thousand frogs raining down
the deluge croaking

43.
bees enter a swarm
the mass shifting like a fog
a floating shadow

44.
through the Grand Canyon
the rapids dance with the raft
tango in the toss

45.
the man is worthy
and carries his honor well
children uphold him

46.
old women are wise
indeed they will tell you so
and gossip goes round

47.
a beautiful girl
flowers in her flowing hair
a petal spins down

48.
a golden eagle
clutching the slippery air
incises the storm

49.
on the barn's red wall
the tobacco's drifting smoke
a rainy harvest

50.
when you went away
I burned sweetgrass and cedar
when will you return

51.
rolling tumbleweed
a globe and brittle network
wayfaring pilgrim

52.
a seductive scent
your hair like the sheen of flax
je suis dans la lune

53.
on the crooked limb
a harbinger of the fall
the aspens shiver

54.
the chill of morning
becomes the September noon
orange, red, yellow

55.
the wind-shaped icebergs
colors ranging on the sea
little auks skimming

56.
the Silk Road winding
ancient towns and rich bazaars
numberless spices

57.
the mother ditch bends
beneath elder cottonwoods
the sun splinters

58.
I follow the tracks
a lean tawny animal
blends in the grass

59.
the flower most loved
beheaded in the bean field
mere execution

60.
the lowly lizard
crouching on the sandy path
claims the right-of-way

61.

the cemetery
row upon row of headstones
a white armada

62.

a pride of lions
in the streets of Nairobi
shops closing early

63.

the perfect poem
in Tibet it is written
and there it is lost

64.

shadows weave and dance
on the walls of Samarkand
where Tamerlane sleeps

65.

in the city streets
the raucous sounds of commerce
silence the outcast

66.
golden birds of prey
the rodent stiff in shadow
ancient sacrifice

67.
in the wild surround
lions in the underbrush
nothing is unseen

68.
cistern in the rain
a feathered migration
descending in thirst

69.
in a quiet room
the retreat of growing old
dreams of days gone by

70.
in a yellow dress
she glories in the summer
and we give good thanks

71.

we speak of spices
hunger has no urgency
fragrances will do

72.

on the trembling rock
I gaze on infinity
waves crash under me

73.

the poet recites
children listen and wonder
these are the first words

74.

the sound of crickets
in the green and yellow fields
strident threnody

75.

the valley below
a song among the shadows
the lyrical land

76.
thunderheads rising
on the far rim of the world
blackness descending

77.
I will wait for you
make a song as you approach
my soul will listen

78.
butterflies swirling
upon the crest of a knoll
clouds of confetti

79.
landscapes forgotten
a return to sacred sites
a world renewal

80.
a lynx on the slope
paw prints tracing a straight line
to deeps in the wood

81.
words marshaled in file
constructions of thought and dreams
miracles of meaning

82.
a bend in the road
the train curls around a lake
the moon divided

83.
the candle gutters
darkness creeps upon the floor
objects change their shape

84.
on the autobahn
flashing lights in the mirror
whoosh a Mercedes

85.
in the great ballroom
a couple comes together
from a single cell

86.
you were sound asleep
the moon slipped behind a cloud
you bathed in blue light

87.
geologic time
informs the towering cliffs
with eternity

88.
a brush on linen
color and image emerge
a village in snow

89.
the river winding
across the yellow expanse
would define distance

90.
a book of poems
arrived in the afternoon
a bound excitement

91.

then a blue aura

surrounded you where you stood

energy of love

92.

one hundred haiku

elemental exercise

to nourish the mind

93.

to invade Russia

in the fury of winter

surely ill-advised

94.

an imperfection

the flaw in the walking stick

a fortune unique

95.

in Brocéliande

in the hold of Merlin's tomb

far from Camelot

96.

the wild mare lunges
and bolts through the arroyo
on the edge of fear

97.

on a green hillside
a man herds his flock of sheep
on an heirloom stick

98.

for the villagers
stories as old as the earth
tell the human heart

99.

in the beginning
the sound of the spoken word
the roll of thunder

100.

in far dimensions
you have succeeded at last
mere mortality

III

There was a woman whose hair was long and heavy and black and beautiful. She drew it about her like a shawl and so divided herself from the world that not even Age could find her. Now and then she steals into the men's societies and fits her voice into their holiest songs. And always, just there, is a shadow which the firelight cannot cleave.

From *IN THE PRESENCE OF THE SUN*

THE DEATH OF SITTING BEAR

There is the photograph taken by William S. Soule at
Fort Sill, Indian Territory, in 1870, a black-and-white
photoprint, 6 x 7 inches mounted on 8 x 10 inches paper
and preserved in the National Anthropological Archives of
the Smithsonian Institution.

Sitting Bear sits looking directly into the camera. He
is an old man, lean, and weathered. His gray hair is loose
and reaches to his shoulders, and his mustache droops from
the corners of his mouth. His eyes are piercing and narrow
and his nose straight and prominent. His cheekbones are
high and pronounced as well, and his forehead generous.
Most remarkable are his hands, which lie crossed on his
lap. They are long and expressive, indeed artistic, as if he
might have been a painter or a musician. The nails of his
fingers are long and surprisingly light in color, almost white
against his dark skin. Befitting his name they resemble the
long ivory-like claws of *Ursus arctos horribilis*. Draped about
him is a buffalo robe, and he wears the bandolier of the
Kaitsenko society, of which he was the leader. The society
was the elite warrior organization in the Kiowa tribe. It
was composed of ten men only. The bandolier has a loop
at either end. The warrior wore one loop around his neck.
In time of battle the other loop was secured to the ground
by means of a sacred arrow. The Kaitsenko must stand this
ground to the death.

The portrait of Sitting Bear is that of a formidable
man, singular and mysterious, one who exists now in
the distance of myth and oral history. The cultural

principles by which he lived without compromise—
bravery, steadfastness, generosity, and truth—have different
meanings and different magnitudes of importance in our
time than they had in his. And so, I believe, does the
concept of death. Sitting Bear lived the whole way of life
he was given and he died the death of a Kaitsenko warrior.
For him that was an equation both proper and inevitable.

O sun, you remain forever, but we Kaitsenko
   must die,
O earth, you remain forever, but we Kaitsenko
   must die.

Sitting Bear, 1870
(*Photograph by William S. Soule*)

1

It was in my name that the blood bore me,
Set-angya in Kiowa, otherwise Sitting Bear.
The hills are black where I was born,
Dark in the density of wilderness, tangled
In twists of pine and oak, floating on the plain.
Below, a prairie tufted in whispering grass, a fan
Of undulant drifts, a bare definition of the earth.
In me a memory of the ancestral north.

2

Origins confirmed me. There lay the hollow log.
And the emergence of the coming-out people,
One by one. From what mythic world did we come?
Beyond the Yellowstone a Sarsi woman and
The Athapascan strain, and I was of two parts,
Waif and warrior in the camps, then sage and chief.
I heard ice ringing on the wind, and beheld the
Shivering colors of the Arctic night, and a destiny.

3

Mine were a people of pilgrimage. On the Great
Plains they followed the arc of the sun. I so
Embraced the meaning of my name. I was brave,
Steadfast, generous, and true. And I excelled;
Honors were placed on me. I led the Kaitsenko,
The band of ten heroes. We owned the death song.
I was known beyond the camps and among enemies.
My medicine was feared, and I taunted death.

4

There were many horses in my herd. On horseback
I rode through the barrier of distance. I was of
The Centaur Culture, drifting on the beat of hooves.
My favorite son, a pipe bearer, was slain in Texas.
I went there and gathered up his bones, leading
A pony that bore them through the camps. At night
I placed them in a ceremonial tepee and called out,
"My son is at home. Come and pay your respects!"

5

Like grasshoppers the soldiers and settlers came.
The ruts of wagons were entrenched in dust
And whirlwinds sundered the vast weavings of
Timber and grass. The buffalo wallows were dry.
Brooding, I held the wrinkled hand of shame.
I mourned the pipe bearer whose bones gleamed
In fire- and moonlight. I stroked the hair of
The pipe bearer's mother, and together we wept.

6

The Kaitsenko warriors were desperate to be free;
In summer, when the creeks were high and slow,
Our spirits were fettered. We craved danger.
There came a wagon train on the Salt Creek prairie,
And we fell upon it. On my hurtful hands were
The stains of blood and blame. I became a captive
And was imprisoned at Fort Sill. Overnight,
In chains, I grew old. My spirit was stolen away.

7

In irons I was placed in a wain, a red blanket
Of the Kaitsenko about my head, and driven across
The fort, an escort of armed outriders on either side.
Singing my death song, I made strong medicine.
Gnawing my wrists to the bone I slipped my bonds.
Blood beaded the bone, the color of watermelon.
I conjured a knife and attacked the teamster.
The outriders opened fire, and I slumped down.

8

There is fury and confusion, then a final calm.
I barely see the cracks in the creaking boards;
They ravel and wave. There comes a shadow
On the sun, and I feel the weight of nothing fall.
I cannot feel the heft of time. The air is empty.
The soldiers take hold of me, bear me beyond hurt.
Their hands are not like the hands of my people.
They cradle me, but they do not hold my heart.

9

In the arrogance of the Kaitsenko I had spoken,
"By the time we reach that tree, I will be dead."
In my stricken mind I dreamed of time, winter
1870–71. In the Set-t'an calendar the drawing of a
Man made of bones and the image of a sitting bear:
My son come home, O my warrior son come home!
Time is a clock at Fort Sill. From a number I come,
And to that number I return. It is a good round way.

10

If death lingers in a dream, let it be a worthy dream.
Let me see my son astride a hunting horse running
Ahead of brave warriors. And let me see him home.
May he and I be remembered in the Sun Dance, and
May our footsteps roll in the thunder of hooves.
And when the moon ascends in the summer night,
May our voices enter into the call of the prairie wolf.
Let our last song drift in the crooks of bright rivers.

11

I become the being I was at the mouth of the log.
Between birth and death is the way of the warrior,
And there is nothing at either end but a dream.
I have lived the whole circle; nothing is left,
And in that nothing is everything for the Kaitsenko.
There is bravery, steadfastness, generosity, and truth.
It is a good day to die, for I have seen the dawn and
Dusk. I have seen high-headed horses racing.

12

In death my hair is lifted on the wind. My blood,
Seeping from my wounds, glistens in the afternoon.
Will strong words follow in my way?—"He died
As his son died, taking hold of the warrior way.
Himself, set against the living tree, is in form
The likeness of a sitting bear." Away in the dusk
There is quiet in the camps. Stories are told,
And a final faint light settles in the silver grass.

NOTE (on Set-t'an Calendar Entry):

According to their origin myth the Kiowas entered the
world through a hollow log. The earliest evidence we
have places them in the Yellowstone country. Sitting Bear
himself is believed to have been born in the Black Hills,
and his paternal grandmother an Athapascan woman of
the Sarsi tribe of western Canada. Clearly he had roots
in the north and took part in the migration of the Kiowas
to the Southern Plains.

The Set-t'an Kiowa annual calendar was painted on buffalo
hide and depicts the years 1833–1892. The entries are
pictographs arranged on a spiral, one for the summer and
one for the winter. The summer is indicated by the form
of a Sun Dance lodge, the winter by a vertical black bar.
There can be little doubt that Sitting Bear knew of this
calendar, particularly the entry of 1871 commemorating the
retrieval of his son's bones.

The tree is no longer on the grounds at Fort Sill. The road
beside which it stood bears the name Sitting Bear.

SET-T'AN CALENDAR ENTRY

Set-ä'ngya Ä'ton Ágan-de Sai, "Winter when they brought Set-ängya's bones."

For this winter the Set-t'an calendar records the bringing home of the bones of young Set-ängya, indicated by a skeleton above the winter mark, with a sitting bear over the head.

In the spring of 1870, before the last sun dance, the son of the noted chief Set-ängya ("Sitting-bear"), the young man having the same name as his father, had made a raid with a few followers into Texas, where, while making an attack upon a house, he had been shot and killed. After the dance his father with some friends went to Texas, found his bones and wrapped them in several fine blankets, put the bundle upon the back of a led horse and brought them home. On the return journey he killed and scalped a white man, which revenge served in some measure to assuage his grief. On reaching home he erected a tipi with a raised platform inside, upon which, as upon a bed, he placed the bundle containing his son's bones. He then made a feast within the funeral tipi, to which he invited all his friends in the name of his son, telling them, "My son calls you to eat." From that time he always spoke of his son as sleeping, not as dead, and frequently put food and water near the platform for his refreshment on awaking. While on a march the remains were always put upon the saddle of a led horse, as when first brought home, the tipi and the horse thus burdened being a matter of personal knowledge to all the middle-age people of the tribe now living. He continued to care for his son's bones in this manner until he himself was killed at Fort Sill about a year later, when the Kiowa buried them. Although a young man, Set-ängya's son held the office of *Toñhyópdǎ'*, the pipe-bearer or leader who went in front of the young warriors on a war expedition.

(Excerpt from *Calendar History of the Kiowa Indians* by James Mooney)

SUSQUEHANNA

Carlisle, Pennsylvania, is a town in which the leaves turn
and fall in October. They scatter and skid in the streets;
they are rolling facets of the autumn sun. The farmer's
market is alive with commerce and music. There are
melons and squash of various stripes and colors. There is
sourdough bread on which to spread brie with threads of
blue in it. Pretty Mennonite girls are about and children
tumble in the grass.

The town of historic significance. It was a munitions
depot in the Revolutionary War and was shelled by
Confederate forces in the Gettysburg campaign of the
American Civil War. It was also the site of perhaps the
greatest experiment in education and domestic diplomacy
in American history.

The Carlisle Indian Industrial School was founded in
1879. Before it was closed in 1918 ten thousand American
Indian children were sent there to be shorn of their native
identity, to be "civilized." The great experiment was a
great failure. Less than one tenth of the students graduated,
many more died at the school, traumatized by disease,
loneliness, and despair. Those who returned to their homes
or who were dispersed into the dominant society were
unable to live wholly in either world; they were dislocated
in their minds and hearts.

The words "sacrifice" and "sacred" are related. The
children whose sacrifice is marked by rows of gravestones

in the Carlisle Indian School cemetery were and are, in their innocence and martyrdom, sacred beings.

I have come to Carlisle to observe the one hundredth anniversary of the closing of the Indian School. Some of the descendents of the students have come as well, and I count myself among them.

The town and countryside are becoming rich with color. There is already a bountiful harvest of pumpkins, and nearby, the Indian river Susquehanna courses along walls of green boughs blushing. There are ghosts. The lost children are like leaves whirling slowly on the bright water. They dip and enter into the mist of time. They are no longer visible, but they are there. They touch the face of eternity.

PIGMENTS

Altamira

On the long littoral,
they grazed in his view,
the rude rounded forms.

He closed his eyes,
and they were profoundly there,
stolid and serene.

He longed to define them,
to lure them into memory
and confirm their sacred being.

He strove for utterance
but had only the language
of signs and pigments.

On the wall of a cave
he traced their existence,
and his hands trembled.

In the vortex of dreams
they crept upon the wall
and the plane of his perception.

They milled before him.
He regarded them and wept,
having been in the hold of wonder.

They would succeed him,
beloved, constrained to his spirit,
and at last given to darkness.

LINGUIST

First the language of love,
Then that of fear, then that of solitude,
Keeping the beat of burning rain.
Lightning glances on the west,
And the soul comes to rest
Among the darker languages.

Silver grain wavers below the hills.
In moonlight there are apparitions
Ranging along a crooked creek,
Leaning into hollows of silence
And waiting not to hear nor to be heard.
The black earth shines in the crack of thunder
That is itself like a rolling language,
Unintelligible, deep in the shadow of distance.

DANCERS ON THE BEACH

The sky lies on the earth at night.
The moon lays on the earth a light

consequential. On the blue sand
are firelit figures dancing, and

their shadows are tentacles bound
among the trees. The brittle sound

of clackers rattle on the beach.
The dancers curtsy each to each.

And in the density of dream
the dancers sway, the breakers gleam.

At dawn the revelry subsides
and there remain the crescent tides.

Slowly the footprints fill and fade
like memories the mind has made.

ULTIMUS

When I have reckoned time and space
And broken from the world's embrace,
Remember what was good in me
And see beyond my frailty.
In all my days I did mean well.
Remember not how short I fell.

THE SPHERES

His soul had approached that region where dwell the vast hosts of the dead. He was conscious of, but could not apprehend, their wayward and flickering existence.

—JAMES JOYCE, "THE DEAD"

They are spheres, you know,
Burnt out and mummified; yet they shine,
And among them we shall make our way.
It is said there is a music. Imagine!
I think that in a fever I have heard it—
A music faint as leaves that twist into grass.
It rings, barely audible, like wind chimes
   across the way.
And we are drawn like moths to the spheres.
The spheres are burnt out and mummified,
And in timelessness they shine! They do shine!
One by one we enter that eternity, remembering
The chimes of mere mortality, and
   fire, then embers, then ash.

A PRESENCE IN THE TREES

What presence in the trees does not appear?
For nothing in the trees engenders fear.
A vagrant shadow in the trees draws near.

ON THE STAIR

Too often has it been too late.
I risk my soul and contemplate

The instant that is lately dead.
I reckon what I might have said

Had I been quicker in my brain
And given words to weave again.

But you are gone, and I am left
To find my tongue at last, bereft.

On these dark steps my wit is keen.
Imagine what I meant to mean.

LINES FOR MY DAUGHTER

Cael. 1962–2017

With reverence for the earth you venture
into vague margins of advancing rain
and behold crystals of the sailing sun.

The clouds weave ribbons of shade and eclipse,
rippling on the colors that compose you,
sand, sienna, jade, the speckled turquoise

of mountain skies. And in your supple mind
there are shaped the legends of creation,
and in them you appear as dawn appears,

beautiful in the whispers of the wind,
whole among the soft syllables of myth
and the rhythms of serpentine rivers.

Once more you venture. The long days darken
in the wake of your going, and thunder
rolls, bearing you across a ridge of dreams.

I follow on drifts of sweetgrass and smoke,
on a meadow path of pollen I walk
and hold fast the great gift of your being.

I will not let thee go, except thou bless me.

THERE CAME A GHOST

There came a ghost in the night,
Having about it a translucent
Cast, a pale radiance of wonder.
Indeed it was illumined within
As by the moon. It spoke to me
In a language I did not know
But quite understood. It told me
That it had once been immediate
In my world and that it had seen
Me walking hand in hand with
A presence bright and beautiful
And illumined as by the moon.
The ghost took my hand, and
We walked by the sea which was
Illumined by the moon. After
A time I realized that the hand
In mine was the hand of a child
And mine the tracks in the sand.

NENETS

I look for them,
And I grow uneasy and impatient.
Was it yesterday or last year,
When the limbs of the taiga
Began to crisp and harden in the cold,
That they promised to come?
Will they approach from a distance
Bearing bloody hides and hooves?

First I will hear their chanting perhaps,
Or the uneven steps of their ritual dance.
And, yes, I will fear them again.
Not now, but in time I will find advantage
In the falsehood of a sign, a gesture
Of welcome, and I will take up with them.
Together we will hunt the dark beasts
That have no words with which to forgive.

Winter is coming in. Soon firelight will glow
In the frosted windows of the village,
And we hunters will huddle and seek solace
In the blue serenity of the freeze.

A MEASURE OF RAIN

In the measure of time
We take unmeasured steps
In the way that rain
Falls upon a flood,
Striking upon nothing
   but itself.
Beads of rain gather
As on the wires of an abacus.
We calculate a random sum
Of which the value is finite,
The unknown infinite.
It is not a matter of time
   but rain.

LA TIERRA DEL ENCANTO

Clouds build on the northern ridge
Where the shades of night grow pale
And there comes a rain like smoke.
The mountains loom and recede. And
Below, the umber plain is a pitted hide.
There the distance of time runs out,
And the mind extends beyond itself.

I have seen in the twist of wind
The landscape severed and heard
The edged cries of streaming hawks.
First light is a tapestry on canyon walls,
And shadows are pools of illusion.
I am a man of the ancient earth
For I have known the desert at dawn.

TO GAYE

Let us go to the dance again.
Let us be given shawls and robes.
Let our children be given names.

You belong to me, and I to you.
See me young and strong again.
I see you as I first saw you,
Fresh and pure and beautiful.
In your soul you are greatly loved.

Let us be alive in our daughters.
Let us walk among the camps
And be at play in our hearts.

JORNADA DEL MUERTO

It is a deep etching of the sun.
It must be regarded in penance,
In the perspective of suffering,
A burning away of green surfaces,
A cauldron white hot in the shimmer
Of mirage. Old men speak of it
With dreadful wonder and respect.

At night it cools in a blue surround
Of celestial light, the distant ridge
Recedes into the pallor of the stars,
And dawn is the blush of a blood orange.
The morning slants on rippled banks
Standing still in the glitter of ancient glass.
A rattlesnake slithers among the stones.

OCTAVE

There have been broken promises, a few,
And semblances of innocence seen through.

And we have taught each other how to be
In circumstances of duplicity.

So we have done. Contrition be our state
And generosity our saving fate.

I wish us well and take your tender hand
As we approach an unfamiliar land.

YELLOW THE LAND AND SERE

Bone the mornings,
Crystal the noons.
Seldom do the rains come
Now that summer rises
From the fields. There are clouds
Above the mountains,
But they do not move or darken.
They take the shapes of fanciful things,
But they do not move or darken.
Rodents thirst and hide from the sun.
Yellow the land and sere.

THE WINDOW THROUGH WHICH THE LIGHT
OF A CANDLE GLOWED

The windows in the Russian village were framed in blue.
I thought there must have been a great supply of blue paint
thereabouts in the early 20th century, for the windows
in other villages were framed in blue as well. Or perhaps
the windows simply indicated the taste of a particular
paint salesman or that of the local magistrate or of the
magistrate's wife. It scarcely matters. The point is, I was
passing by the village on a late afternoon in winter. Snow
was deep, and the houses and sheds and barns seemed
huddled against the cold, and animals stood still here and
there in an attitude of sheer endurance. Darkness was
approaching, but for a few moments the village stood
against a brilliant sunset, orange and red and magenta.
It was a scene of intense beauty and transformation, not
unlike a painting by Boris Chetkov. It was a study in
evanescence. I paused to take it in, to catch my breath.
Then, as the sky faded, there appeared in the foreground a
window through which the light of a candle glowed. It was
nearly ineffable in its rustic warmth and dignity. It was a
barely visible icon to grace the invisible spirit.

TORRENT

In the late afternoon
In the far end of the canyon
A storm arose. The summer sky
Curdled and piled, and the leaves
Of cottonwoods began to quake,
And there was a rush of the wind.

There came the near edge of darkness,
Then suddenly the drumming of rain
On the river. The burdened air hung
On the great faces of the canyon walls
And turned from ruddy and bone to
Ochre and slate, and then were lost
In a shroud of roiling mist. Brilliant
Bolts of lightning struck along the rims,
And thunder crashed and rolled.

The world was frightening and full of
Havoc, like the breaking of Creation.
Animals cringed in the fury of the false night
And could do nothing but endure, huddled in
Dread and the hold of unknowing.

At last the sky cracked open and the
Setting sun appeared, dropping amber crystals
On the needles of evergreens. There was
Then only the gathering of a clear dusk
And a silence on the ancient walls.

RECONCILIATION

We have no food for fighting.
We must drink the broth of bark
And say kind things to each other.
We must be peaceful. You must say
That I cut a fine figure among men,
And I must say that you are a
   handsome woman.
In this way we shall drink bark broth
And pity those who have food
   for fighting.
Let us sit now in the porch swing
And dangle our feet in thanksgiving.

A MYTHOLOGY OF BELIEF

Did not the king believe
In the reality of the stars?
Or were they merely points
And patterns of mystical illusion?
The evidence of being was compelling.
He could see them, after all, and
He could hear the silence of their pulse.
And was he not named for Arcturus,
The Guardian of the Great Bear?
Some of his relatives may indeed
Have settled among the stars.
Therefore the king must have believed
In their far, flickering existence,
And he must have borne in his mind
A grave mythology of belief.

NORTHERN DAWN

Cold is general on the winter plain,
And an ice fog rises from the crusted snow.
In the village fires burn, and meat is roasting.
In the meeting house elders sit at the walls
And receive food in the season of hunger.
A file of men dance in the hold of trance
And cut their hunters' eyes into the dim
Corners of the Arctic night.

A woodsman enters, rude and grizzled.
He is accustomed, and welcome is accorded.
It is said that he has passed into legend,
Borne by dogs and the glow of constellations.
Indeed his tenure was earned long ago
Along frozen rivers, in slanted crystal fields,
And in the density of dark woods.
Now that he has touched the rim of eternity,
He is at ease, and he nods and dreams.
His hermit soul resides on the outside,
And outside the spirit lights hover and hang.
In the recession of stars the northern dawn
Appears, and he names the wilderness.
He sings among the ravens and the wolves.

THE PILGRIMS

They go, and nothing succeeds them.
In the long distance they disappear,
and where they were there is only
vacancy, the distillation of loss.

In memoriam they walk to no destiny.
Theirs is the burden of pilgrimage.
Their crooked file is etched on planes
of ice, a trace ascending beyond time.

BABUSHKA

1

The Russian woman
Of ancient soul;
In her nature discreet,
In her manner brusque.
She would be kind,
But nothing has prepared her.
She holds in her hard hands
The insistent pain that long ago
She placed among the first
Spring flowers at the Kremlin wall.
And now again she holds the pink
And white blossoms close
To her hollow breast
And whispers thanksgiving.
She lifts her closed eyes
To the March sun.
She has been broken
And mended many times.
With her brush broom
She sweeps the walkways
In the Alexander Gardens,
In her heart are the few shards
Of a child's voice, scattered;

Silently she speaks his name,
And as the daylight darkens
She forgets how to weep
And imagines cabbage soup
And the beat of a linnet's wings.

2

Once she dreamed
Of windows glowing bright
In the great country houses,
Of dancing and laughter
And lilting conversation
That carried elegantly
In the treasure-filled rooms.
With only partial understanding
She kept the tinkling syllables
In the trove of her mind
As if they could not be heard again.
In her girlhood she dreamed,
And she grew old.

3

Time touches her brain,
And the everyday sight
Of the red Kremlin walls.
The walls become to her
Other than mysterious.

Even the great golden domes
Within are mere glitter, though
At infrequent moments
A dilution of pride and pretense
Moves in her blood, and
She labors on to some beyond
In which first flowers,
The whir of a bird's wings,
And the March sun sustain her.

4

In the forenoon a mother
And her child stroll
In the Gardens. In its pram
The child wriggles and coos,
And the mother dotes.
She is prim and fashionable.
At the wall an army officer
Snaps instructions to young men
Who will execute precisely
The Changing of the Guard.
Across the way an old woman,
Bent and anonymous, swings
A brush broom methodically
back and forth.

A WOMAN WALKING

Had she been poured
into a mold
she should break away
with this much will and grace.

The white sails rise
from the bay.
They seem still against the
motion of the waves.

She walks on the beach
holding a music in her mind.
The sun touches her, and
she regards the distant fog,

Then there is a dead fish.
It is foul and prehistoric.
The woman wishes
she did not know of it,

But in an instant
she had got it caught
behind her eyes, and
she walks quickly on.

SEAMS

The image:
Bees entering the swarm.
The convergence is obscure
As once I saw leaves
Taking hold of the wind
In connection so fine
As to be indivisible.

A hurried cloud,
The swarm shifts and drones,
Gathering density to itself.
The leaves spin and roll,
Edging the air,
And there comes among them
A precise confusion,

And to the margin of a wood
A transparency like rain.

GAMESMEN

What happened to the men who ran
Over and through and all around?

Did they not finish who began
The game to which they were so bound?

How could they have withdrawn from sight?
I love them now as I did then.

They kept the field where might was right
And they were more than mortal men.

They imaged greatness to a child;
Let not their image be defiled.

PRAIRIE HYMN

As my eyes search the prairie
I feel the summer in the spring.
              —CHIPPEWA

On the tongue a hymnal of American names,
And the silence of falling snow—Glacier,
Bearpaw, Bitterroot, Wind River, Yellowstone.
I dreamed among the ice caps long ago,
Ranging with the sun on the inward slope,
Down the wheel of seasons and the solstices
To the tilted moon and cradle of the stars.
There was the prairie, always reaching.

Time was sundered, and the light bore wonder.
The earth broke open and I held my breath.
In the far range of vision the prairie shone bright
As brit on the sea, cresive and undulant.
Antelope bounded and magpies sliced the air.
In the middle distance grazed the dark eminence,
The bestial heft on cleft hooves, the horns hooked.
Oh, sacrificial victim, your heart is sacred!

The range of dawn and dusk; the continent lay out
In prairie shades, in a vast carpet of color and light.
In the Sun Dance I was entranced, I drew in the smoke

Of ancient ice and sang of the wide ancestral land.
Rain-laden clouds ringed the horizon, and the hump-
Backed shape sauntered and turned. Mythic deity!
It became the animal representation of the sun, and
In the prairie wind there was summer in the spring.

ACKNOWLEDGMENTS

The following poems in this volume have been previously published in earlier collections by N. Scott Momaday. Grateful acknowledgment is given to the University of New Mexico Press for permission to reprint them.

"The Kiowa No-Face Doll," "A Sloven," "Division," "Spectre," "The Snow Mare," "The Bone Strikers," "A Silence Like Frost," "*Sobremesa*," and "Before an Old Painting of the Crucifixion" from *Again the Far Morning* © 2013 by N. Scott Momaday. Used with permission of the University of New Mexico Press.

"The Great Fillmore Street Buffalo Drive," "*Nous avons vu la mer*," "On the Cause of a Homely Death," "The Bear," and "Angle of Geese," and extract from "In the Colors of the Night" from *In the Presence of the Sun* © 2009 by N. Scott Momaday. Used with permission of the University of New Mexico Press.

"Yahweh to Urset," "To an Aged Bear," "Prayer for Words," "The Blind Astrologers," "Revenant," and "Meditation on Wilderness" from *In the Bear's House* © 2010 by N. Scott Momaday. Used with permission of the University of New Mexico Press.

ABOUT THE AUTHOR

N. SCOTT MOMADAY is an internationally renowned poet, novelist, artist, teacher, and storyteller. A member of the Kiowa tribe, he has dedicated his life's work to preserving and celebrating Native American heritage and the oral tradition. He won the Pulitzer Prize in 1969 for his first novel, *House Made of Dawn*, and is the recipient of numerous award and honors including a National Medal of Arts, the Anisfield-Wolf Lifetime Achievement Award, the Ken Burns American Heritage Prize, and the Dayton Literary Peace Prize Ambassador Richard C. Holbrooke Distinguished Achievement Award. In 2021 he was awarded the Frost Medal for distinguished lifetime achievement in poetry. A longtime professor of English and American literature, Momaday earned his PhD from Stanford University and retired as Regents Professor at the University of Arizona. He lives in New Mexico.

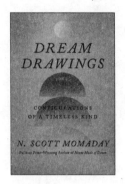

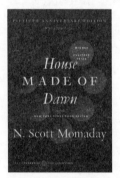